Vanilla Paper and Other Tragedies

By Lunar Patni

To everyone who tried to make me feel worth it
And to those who made sure I didn't

Charcoal Hair

I run a hand through my charcoal hair
I blink the tears out of my dirty eyes
I pick the skin on my caramel arms
I fight the thoughts in my weighed brain
I freeze as I hear the poisoned yells
I'm chased by the monsters and their sharp teeth
and i hide from their sharper words
I hide in the cell i call my own
I hear the voices beyond the barrier
I hear bangs and thuds but I don't unlock
I hide in the room I call my home
I talk to the voices that aren't there
I ask them not to leave me
the voices leave but the monsters don't
cries and screams of agony are heard but I don't give in

I see a silver shining square
shimmer in the fluorescent light
and I press it against my flesh
I shut my eyes and count to three,
bracing myself
the silver turns red
A pool of wine surrounds me
my charcoal hair is brushed back
my dirty eyes widen in shock
my caramel skin in stained in blood
And the thoughts in my brain have won.

Honey

When I talk about you, compliments
gush out of my mouth.
they pour like a bottle of honey
now my bottle is almost empty
you squeeze and squeeze until only
drops are left
and even then you hit the bottle,
wanting more
you long for more honey but there
is never enough
so you buy another bottle.
You long for nectar like a
hummingbird
you envy them, for they can fly
backwards and you can't
so you hit and hit the bottle,
wanting more
but the bottle has gone dry
and so has my heart.

Flame

You are my flame
I feed you my love so the blaze grows higher
But you abuse and abuse
Like a hungry child, you're always greedy for more
Until I have nothing more to give
I try to extinguish you but to no avail
You devour the poison and use it yourself
There's no way out, but do I really want one?
The flames grow higher, riddled with desire, and now i'm melting away
You used to be my Flame
Now you're a pile of ashes.

Comedy

Comedy used to be telling jokes
Now I'm the joke.
People look at e in the halls and laugh
They spit poison at my face and **laugh**.
And if i don't laugh along they laugh more
But i don't understand
They double over, giggling and snickering
And i wish for once i'd get the joke
But that's the thing about comedy
Not everyone gets the joke.

A Sea of Faces

In a sea of full of faces I swim in search of you
My eyes scour the waves of people, looking for my favorite
Finally, I made contact.
I smile
You look away.
A sea full of faces and i'm drowning
And **that's** when you look at me.

Tired

My eyes flutter as i make a weak attempt to stay awake
"Stay awake"
I hear myself mutter
"Eyes open."
The minimal hours of sleep i obtained don't seem to help as i manually struggle to be aware
My head bobs as i attempt to regain consciousness
My brain finally loses as i submit to the strange realm between consciousness and sleep
I can hear my surroundings but my thoughts are gone as i finally let myself "sleep"

Your eyes

On may fifth i met you
We sat together but i never noticed your eyes
That was the day i noticed
Your eyes burned like a thousand suns that day and ripped through my heart
Your eyes remind me of woods on a foggy day
When you're out exploring and you notice the sullen yet somehow warm bark of the trees and something comforts you but you're not sure what
Your eyes have become the headphones that shield my ears from the crowded halls
Or the hand that wipes my tears when i cry
Your coffee brown eyes are pools i drown in
I'm lost and your heart is the map to the depth of your eyes
I'm lost
Doomed to wander forever

For the love I have for your eyes is but a fraction of the love I have for you, but still more than yours for me.
I'm lost in the the caramel swirls of your eyes and i'll never get out as long as your love is the key

Wax

I light up my lighter but never to smoke
But to do something that makes me a joke.
I set a candle on fire as the flames grow higher
And the violet envelops the crimson.
The candle is pink and striped with white
And casts a yellow shining light.
Wax pools in a lake below the wick,
Getting to the brim and making me sick.
I tilt the candle askew so it aligns with my hand
It drip, drip, drips, on my command.
I hiss out in pain but it helps me restrain
From doing something completely inhumane.
But was isn't bad enough to be something serious

And wax isn't sane enough to not
be called delirious
So i sit in my room and i drip the
hit wax
Till i fall on the floor
And I finally collapse.

I hate being trans

I hate repeating my name
i hate cutting my hair
I hate it when people tell me
"they wish they had my chest"
and i hate it when people say to
"look my best"
but my best isn't a suit and tie
my best is a dress.
i hate looking at people and
thinking "i wonder if they'd be
into guys"
i hate looking at boys and
thinking "I wish i was him
sometimes"
I hate feeling unsafe in my body
like watching a scary movie and
wanting to turn away
wanting to turn it off
but you can't.
the tears i cried when i realized
id never be the same
because i'm not a girl.
no, not with this name.
I hate living in fear of being
shot when i go outside

i hate the world i live in
and I hate myself.
and I hate being trans.

And so I left.
And the only one who noticed was
my dog.

Star

I am a star.
Not because i think im amazing,
Quite the contrary actually.
I am a star because I'm only visible when you want to see me.
I'm always there, but only seen when you want to see me.
I am a star because it looks like I have hundreds of thousands of friends, but I don't.
They're hundreds of thousands of miles away.
I am a star because i am mistaken for a planet, when in reality i'm "just a star"
I am a star because I'm supposed to be in a group making a beautiful picture, a constellation, but I'm not.
I'm just a star.
Just one measly star out of billions.
I hope one day i'll find the person who looks at me like how i look at stars

But until then it's me and the stars.
And if i'm lucky you'll be looking up at me someday.
The dullest star out there.

The Moon and I

Every night I look up at my
friend, the moon
I talk to her about you
And I hope you do too.
She listens to me
I hope she listens to you too.
She smiles when i talk with her
glimmering crescent
And she's whole when i cry
So she can show me the light
We don't talk face to face
You ignore me online
But I hope we can talk through the
moon.
So you talk to her
And so will i
And one day your face will replace
hers

Body

When you touch me i beg you to stop
You tell me it's not a big deal.
I fight and i punch
so you take away my arms.
I kick and punt
So you take away my legs.
I look away but that won't do
So you take away my eyes.
I try to tell someone
And there goes my voice.
So i lay there, no arms no legs, no eyes
No mouth or voice, just a head of lies.
I lay there as you touch me and call it a joke
As my body melts away
And my tears make me choke.

Snowflake

When I walk in the halls people call me snowflake.
They call me that because i'm sensitive
They're not wrong.
When people yell or call me names my snowflake starts to melt
My counselor tell me to look on the bright side, im unique in all my ways
But since i'm a snowflake the light hurts my eyes so i hide away
If I really am this unique, surely they know that I am lonely?
To never find someone just like you to relate to all your struggles
When i slouch down the halls people call me snowflake
I'm melting.

6/12/23

June 12th 2022
A stormy day.
The weather was sunny, the sky was smiling, but there was a storm in my head
I took some pills.
A lot of pills.
And wished that i would die
I was tired and stumbling like a drunk, barely able to stay awake
Falling with no one to catch me
I fall into the dark abyss
I didn't die, to my regrets, i couldn't pass the gate
So i'm here on this earth, miserably
Sentenced to witness my fate.

Sorry.

I'm sorry i stubbed my toe
I'm sorry i broke your vase
I'm sorry i said i loved you
I'm sorry I laughed in your face.
And i'm sorry for getting mad
Even worse for being sad.
I'm so sorry i stood up for myself
And i'm sorry you saw me cry
Im sorry im a waste of time
But I know how to make it right.
Even that, I can't do correctly.
So i'm sorry i climbed up that building
I'm sorry i stood up there tall
I'm sorry that when the ambulance came
You were late for work.
Im sorry, i'm so sorry
But i'm gone now so you ca be happy
But even that didn't work.
Stupid
Stupid
STUPID.
I'm sorry.

Blade and Blood

The blood was drawn too early from
his deep mousse skin
The blade's dance was premature on
the nine year old's chubby arms
The waves of sadness washed over
the child until he drowned
The blade and the blood won't
leave the child
Caramel arms turned black and blue
Leave this child alone, please!
Sometimes none is better than one.

Philophobia

Philophobia is the severe fear of falling in love.
As bad as it sounds, I could learn from it.
It happens so fast and new crushes rush at me like a tornado
Love is a trust fall but you don't even know if there's anyone there
I don't trust people.
I don't trust love.
And I don't trust myself.

Broken Raven

I am a raven with a broken wing.
My wings are supposed to be what makes me beautiful
So what do I do without them?
I bathe in the sunlight to see the rainbows dance on my feathers
I am greeted with nothing.
I jump to the clouds to flutter my wings
I want to be unique but I can't.
Why?
I want to be unique
I want to be interesting
But I'm not.
And I can't change that.
Broken wing
Broken raven.

Forget-Me-Not

Please don't forget me.
When were out at a movie or when were apart
When you're out with your friends and i'm home alone
When you're ignoring me or when i'm sad
When you stop talking to me
When you find someone new
When you decide i'm not worth it
It's ok.
Leave me, think of me as the devil, I don't care.
Just don't forget me.

I wish I was dead.

I wish I could run a blade back and forth over my arm until it falls off.
I wish to feel the pain of my arm splitting in two, not unlike my heart.
I wish to watch each layer of my ski split and peel apart until I reach the bone.
And even then i'll take a saw and chisel myself away until i shatter and the shards flow into my bloodstream

Icarus and the Sun

The story of icarus is plain and simple
A boy was given power and abused it.
But what if it wasn't all that simple?
I like to believe that Icarus was a boy who was just that-
Just a boy.
The sun was a slightly younger youth
Icarus loved him and flocked to bask in his light but he lost himself
The sun had the moon.
And in the pain of the loss of his first love Icarus flew to the sun
But not to show off, no.
He flew to spend his final moments with the sun
He was just a boy
Just a lover
Just Icarus.

Konoronhkwa

Almost a year ago my lover left me
To me he'd say Konoronhkwa.
"Konoronhkwa, Lunar!"
He'd say.
When i laughed
When i cried
Even when I just sat there.
"Konoronhkwa, Lunar."
And he'd wrap me in the blanket of
his words and I'd smile and feel
my face go hot like I was baking
in an oven to a crispy golden
brown.
I'd laugh.
"Ti amo, [redacted]!"
Id smile and blush
Forever and always.
I always thought it was silly when
he practiced on me,
Stuttering to learn a new language
to love me in.
Now that he's gone I don't think
it was so silly.
Konoronhkwa, [redacted].
Forever and always.

Penguins

Penguins mate for life.
The male lays a pebble at the females feet
If or when she accepts, they are bonded for life.
I wish i were a penguin,
At least then I'd have a mate.
But even then i'd be te spare penguin
Chubby and tattered.
It's sad when a penguin passes,
but not this one.
This penguin has a disheveled look
Tired eyes, and a mountainous beak,
Scruffy fur and bumpy skin.
It's chubby and ugly and laughed at.
When a penguin dies there is clear mourning
So then why do you encourage this one's death?
Good riddance, little penguin.
I know it's not fair
But i'll soon see you in heaven
Farewell.

Butter

The amaranth wine spills from my
hickory skin as dirty white lines
appear
The skin surrounding the lines
turns purple
It swells up like a puffer fish
The wine continues to spill from
my wrist
Tissues turn crimson and pools you
can swim in form under me.
The skin splits open like silicone
The way it slipped through my
wrist with ease,
You may as well have called me
butter.

My Rose

Stunning
Absolutely breathtaking.
You are embellished with bubblegum pink,
The same color that scatters my cheeks when you are near.
Roses dance across your torso
Intertwining stems brushing their leaves together
I wish those were us but it can't be
You're all petals
I'm all thorns
So as much as we try, we're just not meant to be.

Classroom Waltz

Pretending to stare at the poster behind you is pointless when you play the same game I do.
I study your cedar toned locks and every once in a while I catch your eyes grazing over my wine and ebony toned hair.
Our eyes meet for but a second before my vision darts away
But youre glued to me.
It's as if you're entranced, like you simply **can't** look away from me,
My prickly skin
My flabby face.
Slowly, cautiously, I sneak my sight back to you but you haven't looked away at all.
You're frozen, starstruck by my greasy skin and mountainous nose.
I look away but I can't stop stealing glances.
Oh, even your name tells me i should look away,
You're named after a lying traitor!

But I don't.
I can't.
You compel me with your frozen eyes
You look away but only for a second before our eyes meet again.
Once our time is up you arise.
The tension melts
The spell is broken
And there is nothing more to it.

And suddenly, I had an overwhelming urge to lie on your lap.

Love to Love

I'm trying harder and harder to convince myself I'm not destined for love.
Every time I catch myself I try to stop because I know I'll just get my stupid heart broken again.
Like always.
I don't have a person to write about as of now,
No one to be head over heels for,
No one im infatuated with
But I don't care.
I just want to love
I **LOVE** loving people.
And even when i try to stop,
That ever existent feeling of a warm chocolate bar in autumn seeps into my heart.
Almost like moonlight sneaking into a locked church at midnight.
I love loving, and I can't stop.
So i suppose love might be real
I'm just not destined for it.
So i'll keep loving
And i'll keep trying to stop myself

And I'll keep getting hurt. And
that's okay.
That's love,

Unrequited, Unloveable

Those who live without love are alone and their hearts are cold.
A quote that's stuck with me for years.
But i'm jealous of those who live without love
For the pain can be too much to bear.
When you find someone and pour your heart into them
Until all your love is dry
But their feelings are hollow
It messes with your heart and breaks your train of thought.
Because when you're unlovable you can't love yourself.
The feeling of rejection and fear washes over you like waves on a beach
It slowly chips away at your self esteem
Chiseling it all away.
Until one day nothing is left but the rotten feeling in the back of your mind.
"I'm unloved.

Forever and always."

I've been shot

I look at him
I look at his stupid grin
God, he really wears his smile
like a loaded gun.
I zone out, and out of nowhere,
BAM!
He shoots me with the bullet of
his voice
And the arrow of love.

For old times sake

"Let's do it one more time.
For old times sake?"
A beautiful, beautiful phrase.
One last time, not for the love we have, but for the love we had.
One final time in *honor* of what once was.
Youre saying you accept the end of this, this-
Whatever we had, and just to make the final time memorable.
You're saying you want to mark our final chapter with a silver lined bookmark on a book,
On **OUR** book that you're putting down for possibly the final time,
But you want to keep that silver lined bookmark on this page, just in case you find our book interesting once more and decide to open it
For old times sake.
You're telling, no, asking.
Just asking.
Just asking to honor our past,

You just want to experience us one last time.
One.
Last.
Time.
For old times sake?

Chicken Scratch

A much as i write
I'll never be a poem
Pretty
Melodious
Put together
Neat
I'm not a poem.
I'm the unfinished rough draft
scrawled in chicken scratch
Never complete
Never published
Just a messy idea in an old notebook
Surrounded by "perfection"

Annotating my destiny

Sometimes I wish my life was a
book.
If life was a book I could take a
small peek at the last few pages
and make sure everything would
turn out okay.
Maybe i could change my past
My future.
I could tear out some pages, add
some more,
I could guarantee id never end up
in a heap on the floor,
Curled up in my cotton cocoon on
the cold tiled floor,
No.
If life was a book ids be happy
and pure
Page by page, I'd be annotating my
destiny.

Default Settings.

Life is a game where God
customizes your character.
I think he shuffled one too many
ties on mine.

Co-dependant

I hold you on a gem studded
pedestal where you sit, sleep, and
dream
You throw me onto a bed of nails
below you and i stay and i worship
you
I don't think I really am anything
without you.
The nails stab me
They peirce my skin
They break my heart
But i love you so much i'll keep
sleeping on my bed of nails
After a while it's not *that* bad.

Spark

I would set fire to the world around me,
Repelling injustice and hate
I would burn down the places that promised to keep me safe but held me up to danger and let it scratch my face
I would let embers kiss the ones who made me suffer, who tried to steal my life
And i'd watch the world burn at my fingertips
But not a single spark would touch you.
Except ours.

Pause. Resume.

I have a strong desire to hit a pause button on my life
I want to hit **X** for a little while and take a breath
The bloodied battlefield needs a break
As do i.
Sadly, my life isn't a movie
No pause button
No happy endings.
But you, my love, are a break from the torn apart ruins of my life.
An oasis in a desert.
The hope in pandora's box,
You fly out and save mankind,
Save me.
But all good things must come to an end,
So you leave
And my life resumes
But i'm grateful
I really needed that break
Thank you, pause-
Nevermind.

Ryan

He is made of weed, brandy, and strong opinions as tough as steadfast as he is.
Wire was coiled to make each separate curl on his head
Topaz crystals stolen from the earth below and placed onto the ivory of his eyes
Rose petals were carefully selected to create his lips
For a split second it was hot enough to melt his stone cold gaze but he regained himself almost immediately
I have faith.
I will slowly chisel and erode his hard features away.

And i long
And i hope
That one day il miraculously bump into someone
And i'll find my beloved
The one.
But somewhere deep inside i know the truth
I'll return home just as lonely as before,
And a little more broken.

Cotton Candy Vodka

Cotton Candy Vodka is sweet and fiery
It burns in your chest like a venetian red african sunrise
A fire unquenchable,
Setting your heart ablaze.
Cotton candy vodka makes you feel sick
It gives you cavities
And makes you throw up
Cotton candy vodka gets you so unbearably drunk that you think to yourself that it might not be the worst drink in the world
Cotton candy vodka is disgusting and just objectively bad.
But what if it can't control how it tastes?
Maybe it wants to be delicious and loves, popular,
A first choice.
Every day, every bar.
"What would you like to order sir?"
And he looks at the cotton candy vodka

And his friends look at him
"One whiskey please."

Cariño

I can sense my face go bright red,
Like rose petals scattering across my cheeks
I can almost feel the heat that swims in your dimples.
But isn't this forbidden?
Will this really happen?
Are you really that insane that you'd ever have feelings for me?
Other than hatred of course.
The way you adorn yourself in mossy, emerald green.
Your dark eau de nil attracts me,
Like a butterfly to pollen
God this is demented!
Are you really so crazy,
So absolutely daft that you'd stoop this low?
But oh..
Cariño, how you look at me.
Maybe i'm imagining this,
But maybe I'm not.
Maybe i have a chance
Give me a chance, just one?

The eight deadly sins

Envy - The green poison that dances in your vision when someone has something you want and lack

Pride - When an egotistical being cares more about themself than others, valuing their devine being above all else.

Greed - Best comparable to a breastfed child. Always whining and begging for more, but more is a construct and is never enough.

Wrath - bottled up, condensed fury. Seeing bright, bloody, red when faced with something not going your way.

Gluttony - Binging. Not being able to stop eating. Continuously just eating, eating, EATING! No viable stopping point.

Lust - The act of giving into your primal urges of mating with another human (or other) for release. Going slowly crazy, your brain and genitals rotting from overuse just to temporarily satisfy yourself.

Sloth - The severe lack of being productive. The dark orchid feel of not being able to get up. The coziness of the blanket as you reduce to awaken.

Love - Insanity. The desire, the **need** to be held and cared for. The lust of the heart and soul, the need to be held like a crying baby, cradled, as the most important person in your life holds you and whispers sweet nothings, ensuring that you'll be okay. The desperation that slowly drives you crazy. Insane. Until your whole life revolves around trying to be loved to no avail. Love. insanity.

The eight deadly sins

All Ears

I speak but no one listens
My mouth is stitched shut
My voice,
once a melody,
Now barely even words.
I beg and plead to be heard,
Just once
Please,
God please,
Just one person
Just listen and make me feel
loved.
Mother, father, just listen to me,
I beg of you!
I need someone to just look at me
and smile
I want to feel their gaze soften
as they listen to me ramble about
everything and nothing
I want them to rest their hand on
my shoulder
And whisper that they're impressed
by work
And proud of me.
I want them to realize how much
those words mean to me

And I want them to cocoon me in a hug as I cry.
I want to be *listened* to.
"Mom? Dad..?"
And my imagination speaks up
"I'm all ears, kiddo."

The stupid boy i like

He looks so stupid.
Stupid sitting by himself
Stupid when he brushes back his stupid hair
Stupid.
I gaze upon his stupid eyes
And stupid lips
And stupid thighs
And for some reason he looks back at me
And he smiles with those stupid lips
I smile shyly at his stupid smooth skin
And somehow his stupid dimples smile back at me.
And i laugh when he makes his stupid jokes
And i blush when he lays down next to me
And in my stupid imagination
I kiss him
And i comfort him when he cries
And he looks at me
With those stupid
Eyes.

Anorexic, healed?

The food touches my lips
I hesitate and open the thin peony petals of my lips
The yellowed gates open
I feel eyes glued onto me as they hear the loud unwrapping of the food
And the crunch as i chew
I feel sick.
Disgusting.
I want to starve myself
I want to deny my body of food and serve it plates of malnutrition
Let me shrivel up to a raisin and have no body
No life
But I'm healed now right?
So i guess im fine

Storm
Inspired by AJB

I watch the sky sob and wail
I watch her yell and scream
I watch the anger flash in her eyes
But she knows everyone is watching her
So she breathes
And pulls herself together
And pretends everything is alright

For you

If your time is borrowed
Let me lend you mine.
If your heart is torn
Let me tape it up.
If your fate is sealed
Let me unlatch it.
If your soul is faded
Let me repaint it.
If your dreams scare you
Let me chase them away.
Let me heal your wounds
Let me solve your problems
Let me love you
Let me in.

Microwave

It will take three minutes and
thirty seconds for your heart to
be ready.
I shove her in the microwave and
wait
I tap my foot impatiently
Maybe if I turn the heat up she'll
be ready faster?
So i turn up the heat
320
350
380
410
And she burns.
I smell the smoke,
Wince,
And try again.
In the trash lies heart
After heart
After heart.

Free bird

Rustic, broken down walls surround me
Moss coats each individual, carefully placed brick
Vines drape themselves along the bodies of the walls
Leaves swoon and throw themselves at the ground,
Creating a yellow brick road for me to follow,
A canary colored blanket to keep the ground warm
I'm completely surrounded.
And yet I have never felt more free.
I feel safe here
I feel at home.

112323

It is Thursday, november 23, 2023
Thanksgiving.
In five days it will be officially one year since we broke apart
And i know you don't care
Or remember
And i know i should be over you by now
And I am!
Kind of.
When i'm feeling really lonely,
Really unwanted,
I look back at us
And what we once were
And I miss us.
I miss us a lot.
I know you don't care
Never did
But it's been almost a year.

Edinburgh

I walked the streets of edinburgh last night
As i stalked the grounds and looked at the brings, colorful, lights contrasting the dark sky, i laid eyes on a boy about my age,
Sixteen or so.
He had light chestnut hair and sea blue eyes glued to a notebook,
Not unlike mine.
I'd like to say he smiled at me and i smiled back, but no
He never even looked up at me.
So i walked the colorful streets and smiled at the boy
Who in turn frowned at his sketchbook.
We never spoke
He didn't even know i existed
But somehow I felt slightly less alone.

Love is Sunday Mornings

Love isn't the person you only take pictures for when you're wearing a full face of makeup and practically nothing more.
Love is Sunday mornings, strands of hair sticking up everywhere
Love is when someone points out their insecurities and you love them, not despite them, but because of them.
Love is knowing their middle name,
Knowing every curve of their body,
Every scar on their skin.
Love is falling and not knowing if anyone will catch you,
Not even knowing if anyone is there,
But still falling.
Love is the feeling of heavenly bliss and perfection whilst running your fingers through their hair.
Love is seeing the love in their eyes be visible every time they see you
Love is comfort

Love is Sunday mornings.

Rubix Cube Aura

For when not a single color fits them.
When you close your eyes and just can't quite pinpoint what color they are.
He's got the passion to be red,
But not the anger.
He's too calm to be orange
Not calm enough to be yellow.
Not green, nor blue, nor purple.
Rainbow is just too neat for him,
One boring, predictable color after the next.
I'd call him my rubix cube
Jumbled up and exciting,
a puzzle to solve.
Ill solve him one day and he'll be my
Neat-but-not-too-neat
Rubix cube.

I wanted to die that day.
But only slightly more than usual.

Elifits

Elifits are the small creatures
that dance through the wind and
change colors every season.
Elicits waltz and tango in the air
They blossom in the spring
Anf thrive in the summer.
In the autumn they change their
clothes into marigolds, monarchs,
Viridian Elifits pull ambers out
of their wardrobes.
In the winter they shrivel to a
prune
And fall to the grounds
And pass
Elifits.
They twirl and play in the sky but
no one acknowledges them.
They fly around,
Hundreds of thousands of them,
Painting the sky embered for only
a second or two
Before falling back to the ground.
When you next stroll outside,
Please notice the Elifits.
Stand for a while and admire them
Before they die for the winter.

So now i sit and wait for a
message
I know it will never arrive.

Oh no.

My phone lays on my lap
No messages
No surprises.
I feel a stray, lone vibration and quickly bring my phone up to y
face
My smile drops in disappointment.
Just an app wanting me to log back on.
I sigh
Then the realization hits me
I like you.
Oh no.

Stranger

I've always been able to tell
who's walking up the steps by the
sound of their strides.
Heavy thuds are my father
Slow, careful steps are my mother
Rapid, childish steps are my
brother
My brother, I don't know what
happened to him.
Now i hear angry thuds,
Not unlike my fathers.
I don't know who walks up this
staircase anymore but its not my
brother anymore
Something destructive has
possessed him
There's a stranger in my house.

Surgery

I don't care that you left me
Well, I do.
But I don't want to.
You try to convince the that i'm
the problem
And I believe you.
But I'm the one who was there
during your surgery.
I'm the one who was there when you
were on the border of life and
death.
I'm glad you survived, really
But I think they messed up your
treatment.
I think they removed your heart by
accident
Or you removed it on purpose.

Human

Human (noun)

1. Not being emotional
2. Killing for own gain
3. Doing anything for own benefit

Synonyms-
- Ruthless
- Apathetic
- cold

Antonyms-
- Kind
- Caring
- Apathetic

Example -
"I hate her. She was great at being human."

Gm

I wonder if i didn't message first,
If we'd ever talk again?
So i dont say my usual good morning
And i wait
And wait
And wait.
Do you even think about me?
Do you worry if you did something wrong if I don't respond?
Do you care?
Does anyone..?
I cave and message like nothing happened
That's probably what you think anyway.
'Gm"
My way of being passive aggressive
No response.

Don't cry

"Don't cry, lunar"
Im told over and over
"Crying is weak,
Do you want to be weak?"
One day i want someone to envelop
me on their warmth and whisper
"You were nine months old.
Cry if you damn want to."

Goodmorning!
Goodnight!
Read 3:27 pm

Clingy

I like clingy

I like double texts and holding hands,
Cuddling and pet names,
Dates every week
Having "our show"
And asking if i ate

I like effort
I love clingy.

I don't like being touched.
I like being embraced.

Writers don't cry.

We are writers
We dont cry
We cut ourselves open and dip our
pens in our flesh
And we write.
We write with our blood,
Our soul
Our heartache,
Our pain.
we dont cry
We bleed on our papers.

I will survive because as long as
i want to die,
I won't be able to.

Snow

I want to call you my snow
For you are beautiful, yet cold.
I long for you but you never come
I should wear gloves to touch you,
But how could i?
I need to feel you, even if it stings.
Your cold skin freezes my flesh and wars my heart
I hope it snows this year.

Maybe if i push you away
You'll finally care enough to pull
me back

Oh.

When I say "oh." I don't mean anything other than ouch.
"Oh." is reserved for when you really, really break, really shatter my heart.
"Oh" means you said something so gut wrenchingly painful that I don't know how to respond.
It means your knife of words has stabbed me right through the heart,
So deep that I don't know how to express it.
So when you told me today that i wasn't your type
Even though i said i was over you,
All i could say was
Oh.

Two Graves

When I die there will be two graves.
One for the me i was,
One for me I am.
When I die there will be two graves.
One for the love my naive self used to feel,
And one for my rotting body.
When I die there will be two graves.
My emotions (we'll call that grave Pandora's Box),
And one for my body,
Just with a simple coffin.

Green

Green tastes like walking into a wooded area and smelling the pure, fresh air
Green tastes like strolling into a forest and spotting a clear lake filled with tadpoles, pebbles, and moss
Green tastes like counting every mushroom you see on every log and occasionally attempting to identify some
Green tastes like looking up and seeing the sun shine through the leaves, as a small azure bird flies overhead
Green tastes like nature
Green tastes like peace.

Im proud of myself
(for once)
And yet i still dont think i a poet
I believe that I am an observer.

The moment i was so sad i couldn't bring any tears to roll down my caramel cheeks
Was the moment i needed to cry the most

Academia

I belong to the nights
I belong to the moon
My home is in libraries
My soul is in old books
And old paintings
When you see the swirls glossed
onto an old yellowed canvas,
Look close and you'll see my heart
and soul.
Every aged typewriter,
Every old grandpa sweater,
Every quill, every inkwell,
That's where I live.
My soul is buried in old academia.

You ask me if I'm okay as I try to hold back the raging river in my eyes and attempt to water the drought in my heart.

There are poets
And there are poems.
She is a poem
I am a poet.

Who I am not

I am not the nine year old who was beaten every day
I am not the thirteen year old who was pinned to the wall and almost raped
I am not the seven year old who was called a terrorist every day
I am not the fourteen year old who was told to strip in front of his [redacted]
I am not the eleven year old who discovered self harm
I am not the fifteen year old whose [redacted] kept touching him
I am not the sixteen year old who is being told to kill himself
I am **NOT** my experiences.
I am myself.

www.ingramcontent.com/pod-product-compliance
Lightning Source LLC
LaVergne TN
LVHW092056060526
838201LV00047B/1416